Spring Journal: Poems

Spring Journal: Poems

By

EDWIN HONIG

WESLEYAN UNIVERSITY PRESS

Middletown, Connecticut

Acknowledgment is gratefully made to the following periodicals, in the pages of which some of these poems were first published: *Chelsea, The Nation, The New Mexico Quarterly, The New York Times, The New Yorker, Saturday Review, Southwest Review, Voices,* and *Yankee.*

The third part of the poem "King of Death" was first published in *Chelsea.*

The poem "November Through a Giant Copper Beech" was first published in *The New Yorker.*

The poem "King of Death" copyright © 1967 by Hallmark Cards, Incorporated.

The poem "Birth Song: in the Wing Seat, at Night" copyright © 1968 by Hallmark Cards, Incorporated.

Library of Congress catalog card number: 68-27540

Manufactured in the United States of America

First edition

For Margot

Contents

ONE

The Dead

You want to bring them back.
Would they, if they could, return,
after such a heavy crossing?
You try, until the wish, almost
disattached, gnawing, growling,
finally bursts loose to call them.

You look up, and they are there:
alert, much younger, fresher, dancing
in the special fragrance
that becomes them, absorbed
in nothing else but this,
this lilt of theirs, their fullest being!

You rush toward them joyfully
when the cry cuts you (is it
out of you or them or whom?),
and you are nowhere, caught and straining
to the faintest, farthest echo
fading,
                    "Edwin! Edwin!"

To Dream

If the eyes want too much to dream,
if the forehead suddenly hit dirt
and the body slackened, letting go,
to lie there actual as stone,

motionless and self-contained,
as though on entering heart's desire
you'd become, as dead, all one,
beyond recall, yet merely slept

like someone who, past wishing, turns
to polar white and heavy animal,
and only this way grows complete —

so to see yourself, flesh of
your dream, your most and solid self,
would you ever sleep again?

King of Death

I.

December winds knock down a shutter. Bronze
evening roughens, rusting toward the town.
Sprung in darkness, he comes alive to search
the lowdown neighborhood for witnesses.

Stretched bare, the ransacked town turns in at nine.
Fire bells halloo him past
the empty depots — feints, beckonings
toward surrender, almost try his mind.

He sees a misty soldier on the way,
warring with rocks on window glass,
fall and crash, the swelling sirens
pouring by him featureless.

Run swift, run slow, in shadow safeties click
on dumb revolvers; his long stretch narrows
down to stand their muzzles' hollowness
before they bellow darkness out.

The papers later said no witnesses
appeared, though faces peered all night
behind the blinds, shifting from TV sets
to nonstop hysterical patrol cars.

II.

After all, he had, and possibly,
when every gobbet's gathered up,
will still appear to have (maimed
man's king of death and poverty)
extraordinary life.

Death is what can die,
in every man, at last.

Awakenings are naked, tremorous,
a waiting to be taken, murderer
or bride, to heart; pursuer sought,
mistaken, shadowing himself;
    feared, a fury silenced,
    darting to sacrifice;
    forsaken, a presence past.

III.

Toward cockcrow, when the inexhaustible poor
lay down and slept, some paid eyewitnesses,
just for the record, detailed an expiration.

They said the howling ceased, a calm descended.
A groggy soldier rose and walked off stiffly
in a borrowed coat. The hill began to shapen

Where the stripped and cornered victim crept,
just as, from his riddled sides, a glory woke
and blazed. It shook, amazing and amazed —

as if enraged, as if it would not die.

Her Hand

She was sleeping an animal sleep
I couldn't make out.
When she woke, the animal sucked,
thinning her face, drowning her mouth.
She drooled and her hand
went at the flecks, vaguely,
purpling the neckskin,
splotched, worn out.
The hand tightening up
went dead on the coverlet.

Dead, but it spoke. It said,
"You will die, you must die."
And I spoke to the hand alone.
"Move," I said. And it moved.
It scurried a bit in the bed,
living a life of its own.
It moved, moving her, not her eyes.
It was hers and not hers.
It was dead, but ordered
by me, it quivered alive.

It didn't want me, it didn't want her.
It had to be what it was without us.
She may not have known it —
squaring herself, almost raising
her shoulders alive,
but the hand, forcing her down,
told her in sleep she would die.
I still follow the end of her sleep:
her animal wide mouth wiped out,
her hand a cinder in the ground.

Eurydice

Can it be?
Looking up from my shoes,
aching,
I see her streaming toward me.
The park is empty.
She is in a wide veil, smoky,
curling,
in a thin blue veil,
whirling.

It is she —
floating by me,
lightening into beauty!
In my emptiness
I rise like water,
bubbling,
breathless to catch up,
exulting!

She turns
a face, not hers,
that balks and crumbles,
whispering,
What are you thinking?
She is dead!

Wind to Wind

In the wind of whoever you are,
the shape that will vanish to be
a smile or a way of holding your head
in the wind of whoever it was
that hovered nearby you is all
that will be of you as you are
when you were least aware —
finger, shoulder, and hair,
full mouth grimacing, forehead surprised,
eye slanted to fondness and hurt,
oh, the lovely fire and cloud of you
burst, hammered and fluffed
through a mind soon to fade
from a body like yours —
your body, my body, all bodies
gathered and thrown in the wind
that widens and thins to air.

Returning to the Old House

This is the house where hurt has faded,
though something lingers, a shucked-off way
of feeling, not yet brushed away.
And I've grown taller watching, as though
mounted on a stump that happens
luckily to be there, and happens,
also, to be me; or I am
both the newfound stranger owner
come smiling through the rooms he'll fill
with chairs and tables of his own,
and the former owner, crouching,
unobserved, still propping walls
and corners with all the forms
he owned and wept and thought.

Do I live dying now with all
those nameless owners who have died
here in this house, once as vivid
to themselves as she who died,
whose hurt has barely left it now?
A full sun stabs the window white,
pours in past my lingering shadow
lengthening down the empty floor.

The Gift

Breaking into the locked room,
he finds a stranger with a baby face
sitting naked, smiling, taking him in,
a pool of blood blanketing his feet.

It is and it is not himself.
It is himself as he might be,
past help, free to turn
to anyone who needed him —

no longer anything to himself,
a scab picked off a wound and ground
into the dirt of every thing.

Free! Free! the round voice sings,
mad as a bell swinging with joy,
then stops. Quick! Quick! before eyes

fail against the final wall, let him
know what joy is, in his heart —
the stranger's heart that eagerly
sang out of him, and stopped.

Back to "Tahiti"

You mean back to where the scarce
old hills and bungled farm and caved-
in barns still sit around the windmill
leaning toward the graybeard house
whose pump is on the blink that has
a swinging handle, long and grim
as the thighbone of a mastodon,
and when the deadman farmer yanks it,
shakes the rust that cakes the well.

That's just where you want to be
when wishfully you say "Tahiti":
back to where you've never been,
you'd let the insidious city rot
with all its piles of cornered meat,
licked by sirens and civilian fires;
let darkness crash on what it will —
the sonic boom of manic jets,
all the blood that's drunk to fill
those weird deserted heads running
bodies that are never still.

But when you stop and listen back,
all is magic, wishful true.
The deadman's breath has just been stilled:
breathing the air he breathed, you stoop
and cut the roses from his bush
beneath the darkened window where
you rise into the view that once
completely filled his drifting eyes.

TWO

For Margot

Almost fallen asleep
in the song of your face,
I tell myself vaguely
to waken and snatch it
at once, so close to
my hearing, or lose it
forever, be lost.

This music that passes·
before words begin
streams through your face,
from the interlocked print
of centipede lashes
to the thinning gold down
ambushing your mouth,

and composes a song
my eyes close to keep
from breathing away.
Should I waken or not?
Enraged by the doubt
I hover, now nearing,
now backing away,

until — what's this?
Your smile wakens eyes,
skies open wide!
Dazzled, still leaning
to hear, my head
drops into its own
Icarus pratfall,

dizzying down
to cacophonous kisses,
in rapids of your
tongue-glistening mouth,
drowning my "Am I . . .
and is this . . . and what was . . .
the song of your face?"

Birth Song: in the Wing Seat, at Night

(for Daniel, born 1966)

1.

See the pink light,
tiny and blinking,
now on, now off,
on a plane wallowing,
a light
swallowed by darkness,
swallowing darkness.

This is my immersion —
I, a traveller,
someone carried,
carrying his blood,
in darkness,
on a plane between lights,
between night and day
(a deathday, a birthday),
travel crosscountry,
wrapped in still air,
knowing only
(through living a dying)
the end will be landing.

2.

Wait!

The end is so near,
it is beginning,
we are beginning.

25

A light is blinking,
pink as a doll.

A child is beginning,
nearing zero.
A starlight approaches.

I am he,
the one thinking,
the traveller.

And the child to be born
(already born,
you will say,
it has happened before),
now waiting
at the end of the journey
is almost here by me.

About me, people, like me,
travelling unknowing
(many men, many women),
waiting to die,
to be born.

The pink light
still blinking up on the wing,
doll-like, in sight,
and starlight approaching,
a child being born.

3.
How shall I know who he is,
now so clearly beside me,

I who am living
knowing I'm dying?

Son! Brother! Creature! Being!
Man dying is
being born!

Over the blinking in darkness
a light, an aura
of fondness is widening.

Soon, my love, soon
as the starlight
approaches and brightens,
let this plane down.

4.
Land hurtles to meet us,
bathed wholly
in blood light.

We land in a clatter of darkness.
The blinking is gone.

Son, brother, child,
alight with me now.
We are carried no more.

See, we have passed over,
newborn.

Second Son Day

(for Margot, mother of us)

On this fleshy pink, too sunny afternoon
I note the riotous control of flowerbeds
in the civil, dogbarking air of Berkeley.

All one's innerness draped everywhere
in punishing detail, externalizing memory
in a climate too favorable for nostalgia.

I close my eyelids from the glare and think
only what I want to think — nothing
unpleasant, nothing too spectacular.

I am forty-seven and the just-made father
of a second son, downy Jeremy, asleep in the portico.
I doze to older Daniel spitting in a rage.

And dream I am the older son who gangs up
on his minute brother, slapping him awake:
"How could you intrude on us, we happy three?

You'll never be the darling I am to them.
I'll see to that. I'll nail you to a tree!"
My eyes jerk open, head pounded by a sneeze.

(A tent of gossamer, striped rainbow or pale bass,
invades the lemon tree, teems down on periwinkle.
Are they bands of feeding butterflies or bees?

Then something like a donkey's half-eaten head,
sunken at the feet of peonies, gets swamped by them,
trickling light like honey from a trough.

Do eyes deceive, focused only on the stuff
one wishes to believe? Well, what of it!
Eyes are the fine beginnings of ideas.

Ideas that may not please. So praise the bees,
if that is what they are, and light, if that's it.
I have mine and they have theirs to feed.)

Bless me, Margot, Daniel, just-born Jeremy!

Nativity

Toward the child came starlight,
the light of the world he'd yet
the light of the world he'd yet
to perceive and divine.

Birds, fishes, and men
drew breath with the child,
as if born again,
the dead moving toward starlight.

"Man is King of this life,"
sang the starlight.
"The hunger for death must die.
Man is divine."

Now birds, fishes, and I
hear our blood sing reply
in the newborn child,
opening the eyes of the child.

Erratum: In this first printing the poem "Nativity" on page 30 was printed with an error. The correct text follows.

Nativity

Toward the child came starlight,
the light of his world and mine,
the light of the world he'd yet
to perceive and divine.

Birds, fishes, and men
drew breath with the child,
as if born again,
the dead moving toward starlight.

"Man is King of this life,"
sang the starlight.
"The hunger for death must die.
Man is divine."

Now birds, fishes, and I
hear our blood sing reply
in the newborn child,
opening the eyes of the child.

Race

I look at you and tremble, smiling.
What are you thinking?
Am I the king your husband?
Some dead fish? Anyone at all?
Do I know you? Say I do.
Do I content you? Often, mostly.
Do you contain me? If not you,
who else would, could or should?

The day jams up with clouds,
far white sails striving
in the bay that sweeps them
out to the dark-mouthed sea.
Coolly in a brown light they will return,
one by one, toward sunset, glistening.
When they return, they will not return.
They will not be the same.

As I love you leaning down on you,
I feel the load I am you feel is me.
So the night blows. September passes.
The bay narrows by an inch of silt,
invisible to passing tenders night or day.
Debris goes by, waste hardens, fishes die.
The scene turns bare and freezes —
loses heart and changes.

Only we two stay the same in loving
what we bear, what we contain.

Back in Bodega

In the downrushing sun
winds endlessly fluent
gigantically crinkle
a spun blond field,
crack leathery strips
off a high eucalyptus,
ride lichen-green barns
over failure of fences
creaking and fallen,
shrink to a whirlwind
past carcass of rabbit,
dismembered sheep
in a darkening grove,
while above and beyond
rides totally clear of cloud
the triumphing sky's
appendage of hawks,
drifting controlled
in the ultimate blue.

Mornings in April and May

In the winegiver's gift freeing sunlight restored
in a ripeness begun with the longer days' light,
in the juice of his tongue-tanging, throat-thrumming fire,
are pulse beats recalling the slower first rounds
of the broad light's wheeling through coolness & heat,
of night & day riding with all the bright kindling
& dwindling of lovers, and moons in their white-
to-blue waning & waxing, of palefire-arching
and blood-falling suns through upstarting bushes
& branches, vineyards & orchards, all quietly
urgent in blooming & greening, and in
their sure aiming, unknowing of fruiting & dying.

Messages

1.

The moon full,
    swimming plain and mottled
      on the western rim,
the sun clear,
    raw lime-yellow,
      coming up in the east,
the sky red-violet,
    turning blue,
      turning pearl,
and the sense
    of weight in both spheres
      at opposite ends
giving the feel
    of a momentarily
      balanced world,
a starless artifice,
    precisely
      vanishing.

2.

In the last snow
two deer appeared
in the dumb meadow,
sharply, at once,
standing as if
they'd always been there,
still as death,
twitching their ears.

3.

It was night and the rain dropped
in wide spaces
and puddles ran on rocks
and the wind took on a shape
with the water,
like a body rushing

over low pillows,
something to be touched,
as if in a dream, a strange
familiar somebody, warm,
and craving love!

Late, Late

In the palehaired fields of August
sunlight gravely brushes
poppies, blackeyed daisies,

rusted roses gallivanting
up an old abandoned cellarway
into the open sky.

A peach tree, hunched and mossy,
hard fruit speckled, stiff,
grows near the absent barn.

Red chevrons flashing,
blackbird gangs swell by.
The titmouse follows idly.

Is it their passing darkens
wild mustard, carrot, parsley?
Is it daylight shadows falling?

A first nightstar trembles.
The sickle moon advances
with a special cunning.

November Through a Giant Copper Beech

This almost bare tree is racing
taut in the wind, leaves flaring,
jet fire fed by a hurrying
keen whistling bird, against

hundred-limbed elephant branches,
steadied in wrinkled gray molten
antediluvian skin,
wrapped tight to stay where it is.

Think of sheer endlessness, beauty
patient in form, forever
uncrumbled between time's nickering
teeth — oh brutal necessity!

Think of the still and the flowing —
Heraclitus's *everything passes,*
the one-eyed conviction against
the rockheaded *everything dozes.*

On this bleary white afternoon,
are there fires lit up in heaven
against such faking of quickness
and light, such windy discoursing?

While November numbly collapses,
this beech tree, heavy as death
on the lawn, braces for throat-
cutting ice, bandaging snow.

Bodega, Goodbye

The wind is not right today.
It mocks the ancientness of beams
upholding this loose porch
that has shaded us all summer.
It makes the old porch shudder
and the termite dirt
leak down, down-down.

The wind fusses and blows wrong.
It makes the baby cranky
who should be sleeping in mild air
out of sun's reach on the crooked porch
by the half-gone wooden railing
where a smoked-out hornet's nest
lines the eaves like false teeth.

Night, and the wind still heaves
and gulps, and flaps the shades.
A nightbird cries as though
nothing had ever lain so still
as boulders in the moonlit field.
I turn over in my sleep
like a basket of broken bones.

Grand Tour — Package Deal

You're feeling free and living abroad
near topaz lakes where legendary poets
swam and drowned, your eyes flitting up
mountain paths, saluted by breezy
ephemeralities, tail flickerings of squirrels
resuming the chase, one after another,
like stripes up a barber pole, going swiftly
past the waxy drippings of the pine gums.

Or you're feeling brusque, knifing into weather,
like a gunboat in a fog, off course, dangerous,
controlled, lit up and witless with concern,
in the dank black night going
nowhere, circling, but steaming on!

Or crunching in snow, looking down at your shoes
that look slow-minded back, stained
at the rims, you kick them — since you must —
as if not belonging to you but to someone
who like you is now returning, puffing home
from this all-day tramp, voyage, flight,
and fall, when your eyes, finally, just
as they hit the pillow, slip quietly out
of their sockets like two used-up flash bulbs.

Sometimes a Soft Voice Is Needed

(for Jerry Rosen)

You'll never make great music.
That's made by someone else —
in another room or house,
another town that's warmer,
maybe in a better time.

What you make is wry.
Sensitive? Oh, yes!
It's got that, plus humor,
even some melody.
But melody is out.

Then, you've got your doubts.
Is it *music* that you make?
Even by old standards,
it doesn't hang together.
It's got no certain style.

And no one ever plays it.
When *you* play it, some smile,
others say, oh yes!
listening for something else —
like Ham, the percussivist.

Now *there's* someone with style.
I bet he'll sting the blood,
get the bowels to roar,
maybe just pinch the nerves,
but his stuff sends you — somewhere.

Great? Who knows, who cares.
Why talk art these days?
Now with so much dying
music's got to shake you,
feel like you're spilling guts.

Ham does that, and Lou Spam
too, also Giddy Goo.
Maybe they're not composers,
maybe they don't like music.
But they split you in two.

You still want music? Well,
take piano, flute and drum,
and smash 'em — that's right. Put
fingers in your mouth and stretch
till blood comes, then just hum.

Ah Life, This Lowgrade Infection

Puts fever in my mouth,
running sore and spittle swallower,
my disposall;
brings the highgrade doctor
on a nighttime call
in a black cape bouncing up my stairs,
his glinting Lincoln
purring by the curb.

Pearly spats perfectly akimbo
he sits kibbitzing,
With all that fat it'll take you years
to waste away (say ahhh); just swill
your mouth with salt water.

Ahhh shut that juicy trap,
and damn those frozen smiling teeth
that don't bite off your tongue,
and the front gate clanking shut
for not slicing you in two,
because your limousine won't accidentally
smear you on the ground,
because your wife won't shoot you
pointblank between the eyes
as you sprint into the house drooling,
Wait till I tell you
about this windy prof
dreaming himself up a fever.

Poor me,
the infection worsens;

we're inseparable.
It speaks to me:
Ah chum, don't fret,
the doc's all wet —
fat or not,
I'll never leave you.

How can I be ungrateful?

Everywhere the lights are going out;
fog on all the windows with its tears.
Everywhere marriages are failing —
only mine alone is happy true.

So darling, come, let's kiss.
A little lowgrade fever mouth to mouth
shouldn't harm a bit —
it goes a long long way;
but don't let that get you down,
because life . . .
ah wife, I love you,
I've got it so good it hurts

(say ahhh) forever.

Cuba in Mind

You think, "I've never lived there.
I could never live there."
Anywhere you live
freedom builds within
or breaks your bones.
You have lived there.
You live there now.
Cuba is home.

Polyglot Israel and Back

August, late *août*, days of the dog.
The papers say it's snowing in *Schweitz*.
But the whole Mediterranean rim
bakes and leaks like a jelly.

Mad in *Yeroosholayem*, hangdogging at noon,
my tongue's on a leash.
Tourists crack Yiddish
like sunflower seeds.

Dry fountain. Dead *kitzel* park.
An Arab curled up like a last year's leaf.

Like a woman who bursts into tears,
I burst through my skin in a lasting sweat.

"How can you be a Jew in that country?"
"When will you come back here to live?"

Weep for me not, o daughters of Zion:
I go home tomorrow, my birthday
(forty-five years of the wars and the deaths),
to *Amerikanismus* depraved.
Strapped in and dozing,
I'm slapped awake by a drink and a steak.
I stick to my oar
like a galley slave
flying El Al to *golos* U. S. A.

THREE

Spring Journal

1.

Suffused by paint-cracking warmth in a steamheated room,
late winter rain
slushing away through the snow, the traffic, the auto horns
bleating and shaking
their cages outside, I linger behind pulled shades
lost in the dumps   .
of my own stock presence; with armies caught stark on the edge
of command slowly tearing
their minds awake, I loll half-dozing, attuned to
the rise of a day
embalming the mouth, muting the whistle of play,
the *twitch twitch* of birds
in the melting boughs of a grimy New England day;
gripped in the bowels
of a gray tabernacular house, I lie photographing
the self — myself,
all selves, bright and to fade, as once Mathew Brady,
in innocent camps
of suffering, snapped the tired grim lounging dying
Blue and Gray.

2.

Gray, executioner's day — except for the gone-
to-work armies, who
can tell time on such a day? — as when minuteless hours
congeal around
the electric lights' dimming, a man being put in a chair
to burn heart and brain,
until anyone moving at all feels the waves of the current,
again and again,

shooting straight through his own newly breakfasted body. Something
hangs in the air
which is moveless, omnivorous, sopping up emptiness, loss:
as though humanity's
power of idleness everywhere pulsed through a huge
neglected machine
whirring and wreathing itself on and on in a noiseless
opaqueness of steam
that declared by its presence the total absence of man.
What lives? Who breathes?

3.

The big city graveyards of motherly-fatherly bones
creep into the suburbs,
and farther, up to, around and way past the airports
where we arrive
faster than sound, breaking the barrier which is
ourselves, the whining
of jets with their canned human loads of pilots and passengers
set up to rise
and fall smiling at death, at the bomb, who light up the panels,
lock themselves in
and drop out, shatter, disintegrate into thin air:
a new way of dying,
just settling down to be filtered into the lungs
of the living below.

4.

The President stands up to hundreds of millions, a dog
among dogs barking
into the bags of their heads (" . . . honor in war . . . "),
lapping their brains;
they listen, they roll on their backs, huffing, surprised,

feel something slip
(" . . . our boys are dying for us . . . "), believing only
something has failed,
like a bad job for too long, or the man who has kept it, vanished,
leaving behind
his family but no other trace, like a dime
dropped in a sewer,
yet this man is also the nation, thrashing, distending
itself until,
no longer a man, it subsides in the dark and becomes
the thing that is gone.

5.

There are ways men think they must be they can never be,
nor even try
to become, which rule them who so agree to be ruled:
by death lure in traffic
each day, by war's death, causeless, a battle of no
excuse, an end
in abstract defeat, by headline, the deadbox clicked shut
against sight of blood
loss, heart loss, bone hacked into the groove of a vein;
or as when a man
lingers on in a monstrous self-reproduction of cells,
still breathing but blind
to his being; or as when a woman gives birth to death,
her own death and
another's which never belonged to life, doubly ended —
the ways men think
they must be, run dead on their feet till sleeping and waking
are the same murder.

6.

The fleece of morning still at the window, the juices
of living run over,
pour out of the shrilling sirens, Come to the fire,
crash the old houses,
wash them away, the indwelling unrecognized dead;
with their bone char
blacken your faces and build you new houses, singing
Great is the flex
of my hand, the leap of my tongue, the sudden cringe
of my sweating brow
alert to the deadening lie, by the cool of my body
nakedness,
knowing itself the start and the finish of goodness,
an only life.

7.

The lessons of time wear out (in time all lessons
wear out) and I
turn back to solicit, incredulous, my own life's
burnt-out years,
seeing only the blinking of shutters on gutted ruins,
the ruins all me.
I suspect this but swear the pictures are false, the negatives
rigged — not by me.
I'm alive — O motherly-fatherly deeds, what have I
to do with thee?
But the thought keeps recurring, the no one I always see
looks too much like me.
To whom need I tell this, whose favor do I seek,
having always known
in my bones the truth of the lie, the hole from which all
my fine words leak?

8.

I find a man sitting inside myself, and leering
pedantically.
I let him. I take on his smirk and voice, pitched low.
It relieves me
to be him — small, ceremonious, hedgy, a stuffy
nonentity.
It is always someone quite distinct, somebody
I can name:
an insolent clerk, ogre lady or punitive person
long forgotten.
Where do they suddenly come from? What dredges them up?
I borrow them
like a dirty old jacket I like to wear because
it's so worn,
so ugly, ill-fitting, and because it becomes me.
As a child I was told,
Don't frown — the look will stick to your face forever.
Look mom, I'm frowning.
Look dad, someone I'm not has really become me.
I'm Lon Chaney,
the hunchback of Notre Dame, the Jekyll devouring
odd Mr. Hyde!
The only nice thing about them is that they're disguises
I can easily drop,
like a secret pride, an attitude I must try out,
then quickly discard
when it gets in the way of — what? my being myself?
That's piously said,
but what is it? The truth is it rankles, this having
to take on somebody
else's old smell, ego-fatuous speech and smile.
It punishes me.

They've gotten the upper hand and I'm fighting them all —
punitive ogre,
insolent pedant, weird little bogies, swarming through
the unkillable dark.

9.

Have you ever been taken for somebody else and felt
the oddness of being,
even briefly, not yourself? Then think what it's like,
being faced with the lie,
officially forged, that you *are* somebody else,
have been for years —
in the files of state officialdom, are nothing
more than a Red,
a rat-nosed hustler who may be expected to sell
secrets to Russia.
Whoever you are with whatever image of self
you've taken and shaped
through the years of depressions and wars and deaths, and living
by whatever view
allows you to practice with grace a personal faith,
imagine all this
erased by the routine act of a faceless flunky,
and thereafter,
for years and years (and, who knows, even still),
you are not only
not you, but a dossier grows in the files on someone
it has been decided
(for whatever reason — a name, say, too much like yours
not to be yours)
is actually you, a someone who may or may not
even exist.

10.

Since you cannot even have met him, you're never aware
of him but when you
are grilled third-degree in melodramatic hearings:
"Did you ever
walk down the streets of M with a Negro?" "Did you
ever know X
or Y or Z?" (All prominent communists.) "What about
Q and R?"
(Two rightist extremists!) "How long have you been writing
to A, B and C?"
(Notorious Spanish Reds!) When you find yourself saying
Never or No,
the routine reply, strange on the lips of the sub-
literate griller,
is cynically, "Don't bother to lie — we have evidence
to the contrary."
This happened unstopped in the forties and fifties; the newsreels
and tapes of the hearings
of Famous Fish Caught with Red Herrings are semi-pop items
among the sophisticates
now when grillers grow smoother, wear college ties,
invite you to dinner,
paying your air fare and hotel expenses, maybe,
then bug your phone
when your wife calls — or is it your Red Chinese mistress
with a Bronx accent?
Instead of a hearing a permanent gray siege is laid
on all innerness.

11.

The question Who is involved — a nameless man,
a manless name,

yourself-in-another, another-in-you, enemies,
friends, the same?
begins a network of fantastic relations to people
(never heard of, mostly)
and to events in the past (fictitious mainly,
or never experienced),
until you become in your own eyes a tale conceived
by an idiot through
the sheerest discourtesy of self-perpetuant bureaus
so certain that real
individuals, issues, ideas no longer exist
they have to invent
artificial ones they can handle — nullities looking
something like you.

    12.
Now the unanswerable question is not who are you
but who made you up?
When you try to track down the source of the Frankenstein ape
they say is you,
you are doubly suspected for persisting to question the matter,
on the assumption,
put simply, that the innocent never cry out while the guilty
invariably must,
until, in secret suspecting everyone you've known
as malicious informers,
the infection spreads — a word or a phrase dropped by yourself
to solicit a clue
incriminates you: whom you suspect suspects you.
In time you grow into
the thing you are not, the fiction-not-even-a-man,
absorbed by the lies,

collective, abstract, a fear-bitten nation creates
in the guise of men.

13.

In mock-epic metre this poetry hobbles on stilts,
in boots, in prose,
to say what it has to say straight before it falls
on its face as a poem.
In this it takes after the latest revived poetic
fashion (old
as late Athens, Alexandria, Rome, Donne's London, Edwards'
and Hawthorne's New England)
of disrobing before disemboweling the conscience in public.
The hara-kirists
are not simply Asian but Puritan Jewish American
Spanish Calvinist
English Greek Russian Irish Catholic Protestant
African Poles.
I, Henny Penny, hurt here, because I swallowed
a piece of the world,
and now I am screaming because in return the world
is swallowing me.
Poet, look to your laurels — if any, make sure they're real —
the world is far nuttier,
drunker, more drugged, more beautiful, vainer, impatienter,
stupider than you.
Be true to yourself, if you can, the world is never
true or untrue.

14.

In *Paterson,* Williams' epic, a line from the Greek
is quoted somewhere,
half defense, half apology: "A deformed verse

for a deformed time."
This much is certain: the sense and the music together
come clear when sense
has the edge in addressing the thinking ear; otherwise
it's a sonic smear.
Go then, my verse, on hobble-stilt-booted feet —
better than no feet
at all to get around with; and please keep in mind
that pathetically jolly
young sergeant having his say in a TV feature
on old Viet Nam,
the happy-go-lucky double amputee thanking
his stars for his loss
because he could now teach the rookies a thing or two
they wouldn't know.
With fight-back American pride he was dancing, this man,
on his own Army-issued
detachable legs. Well, out of that viewing came bounding
this ill-natured poem
called "Mouths," recalling the other wars when amputees
weren't so lucky.

    15.

Mouths

Hear us, we are young again and about to die.
There is a war again, and we, who were there before,
dream we are being given over to it,
even as our hearts rebound from it,
unspeaking, sickened, with the strength
of all our separate huge unwillingnesses,
our hundred-million-minded backward dread recoilfulness,
carried now, despite ourselves, squarely into it.

Suddenly the ground is cleared,
dug up for a moment and cleared a bit,
so the amputees may dance alone,
each with his own lost limb,
so the fullbodied may open their hungry jaws
to take in the muck, the sweet muck they died in.

Believe us, no one wants to return.
We are only here dreaming to be a while
with our own cut-off limbs, our cut-off lives,
our long unspeaking mouths telling:
We were as you are now,
living, seized, and drifting,
we are as you will be,
resisting, unremembered, dead.

16.
To the fall of the retching *stump stump* impersonal Anti-
Personnel bombs
instructed, Careful what you hit — nothing personal,
unless it's enemy,
the Voice of America swings into the jungle village.
It's the daily news
coming loudly and clear over the sleek little shortwave
G.I. radio.
"Recognizing his continual unflagging efforts in the cause
of world harmony,
this group of old veterans and soldiers at home have given
the U. S. President
their Special Peace Award." Applause turns to radio
static forever,
since No Person's alive in the village, including the No One
who turned it on.

17.

Brute, wise man, ogre, and beauty, cripple and President;
infant, dwarf,
and pygmy; dotard, darling, enemy, friend,
intellectual giant;
ancient Egyptian, Lestrigonian, Socrates, Moses,
Marx and Hitler;
the wife you sleep with, the mother and father you no
longer live with;
the son you know from the cradle, the fool and the bore
you know at a glance;
all wear inside them — who can tell why or how? —
an all-covering "I,"
an all-weather voluminous self that begins with the fetus's
first flimsy heartbeat
and stretches on out to the last inaudible fall
of the pulsing brain —
everyone that has ever lived, since mankind began,
has worn inside him,
indelibly fixed, an unchangeable picture of exactly
the person he is,
like the silhouette ivory cameo piece grandma wore,
having inside it
the prize tinted portrait of her as she was at sixteen —
and which, whether looked at
or not, each one of us, secretly bearing, regards
as the "real me."

18.

You can't give it up and live. You may drive yourself mad
trying to do this.
Today there's a growing fashion, not yet a rage,

to give it away,
exchange it, or squelch it forever while staying alive:
the acid LSD,
the bodies that tear off their skins to become all soul,
the howling drive
to break down all barriers standing between the inside
and outside of things:
by speed, by brainwave, through space, preventive wars;
harrowing hell
appeals to the mind that likes to play God for some reason;
Dante and Christ
succeeded, each in his permanent way, but the story
is they came back.

19.
As spring comes back each year with its new work and cares —
a breaking of hardness
never repaired or repairable, season of ooze,
of uneasy lures,
into wild air where streetcries and birdcalls ascend
like darting balloons;
into the lilting of summer robing, disrobing, which
people past thirty
no longer feel as a call in the blood (Do people
past thirty plan
all the wars?), the peeling of skins, mutation of genes,
degeneration
of bones, in the garden weeds rampantly growing, shooting up
even through asphalt;
comes the asking of who will survive into summer with nothing
itself but the self
palely regarding the natural unselfregarding
fornications

of objects and bodies . . . cries in the air . . . artilleries . . .
gouging of wounds . . .
rich blood caking where dead men no longer lie . . .
cattle peacefully drinking
at home, in Vietnam . . . and in Teotihuacán,
drawn on a pillar,
" . . . a jaguar singing . . . under his mouth, water; . . . a priest wearing
the robes of a god."

20.

The natural conservatism of thought in the human animal
must have something
to do with the body's unthinking lunge toward survival:
in spring we think
of summer's being, suns' endlessness, bushy stillness,
and stealthily,
as gold pears pull down their boughs, the sudden long
incoming fall.
And so, to keep this from stopping, to welcome all signs
of something ongoing,
as if to say, in a hushed voice's prayerful charm wish,
I'll be alive
wherever there's living still going on, I wrote quickly
this poem called "All Summer":

21.

All Summer

Why does the Princess stand looking away toward the brook?
The Prince needs her. "I am your fate," says a voice from within.
The flowers he tended for her all nod with their flametips.
Neither dares move. "Come closer — " Neither has spoken.
If she spoke — "I cannot believe you would want me — " that's
Where her voice would falter, not with compassion or loneliness,

But with revulsion; so, not to be misunderstood,
She'd have to swallow her feelings and quickly continue,
" — you'd want me to look at you, crippled and putrid, again."

She says nothing to him, still gazing toward her and pleading,
Pleading — when will her great green eyes accept him and when
Will her tissue-blue silks move near him, her hand ever touch him?
Though neither has moved and nothing is said between them,
The air trembles — is it her loathing or his desire?
The flowers bend — is it in pity for him, their gardener,
Or in shame for her silently scorning him? Soon they will wilt.

Soon they will die and soon there will be no garden.
The Prince has turned into a statue imploring the air
With hands cut off at the wrists, neither bone nor marble.
Birds roost in his huge curly head and splatter his shoulders.
Having scampered away, the Princess is now somewhere else
Combing her thick auburn hair, the Prince long forgotten —

Or will she remain to turn into (perhaps is already
Becoming, and is this why the Prince importunes her?)
That dry, almost leafless old crone of a tree by the brookside,
Standing apart in the garden, infested with larvae
Swinging great nets of gossamer hair in the breeze,
The breeze that will shortly become a strong wind, a wind
That will topple the Princess, turn all of her up by the roots
That soon as they crumble, the brook carries off to the sea?

22.
High noon. It's time to get up — jump into my pants,
run out and dance
in the foggy streets of Providence, play God —
maybe bring out the sun!

63

Distinguished contemporary poetry in cloth and paperback editions

ALAN ANSEN: *Disorderly Houses* (1961)

JOHN ASHBERY: *The Tennis Court Oath* (1962)

ROBERT BAGG: *Madonna of the Cello* (1961)

MICHAEL BENEDIKT: *The Body* (1968)

ROBERT BLY: *Silence in the Snowy Fields* (1962)

TURNER CASSITY: *Watchboy, What of the Night?* (1966)

TRAM COMBS: *saint thomas. poems.* (1965)

DONALD DAVIE: *Events and Wisdoms* (1965); *New and Selected Poems* (1961)

JAMES DICKEY: *Buckdancer's Choice* (1965) [National Book Award in Poetry, 1966]; *Drowning With Others* (1962); *Helmets* (1964)

DAVID FERRY: *On the Way to the Island* (1960)

ROBERT FRANCIS: *The Orb Weaver* (1960)

JOHN HAINES: *Winter News* (1966)

EDWIN HONIG: *Spring Journal: Poems* (1968)

RICHARD HOWARD: *The Damages* (1967); *Quantities* (1962)

BARBARA HOWES: *Light and Dark* (1959)

DAVID IGNATOW: *Figures of the Human* (1964); *Rescue the Dead* (1968); *Say Pardon* (1961)

DONALD JUSTICE: *Night Light* (1967); *The Summer Anniversaries* (1960) [A Lamont Poetry Selection]

CHESTER KALLMAN: *Absent and Present* (1963)

PHILIP LEVINE: *Not This Pig* (1968)

LOU LIPSITZ: *Cold Water* (1967)

JOSEPHINE MILES: *Kinds of Affection* (1967)

VASSAR MILLER: *My Bones Being Wiser* (1963); *Onions and Roses* (1968); *Wage War on Silence* (1960)

W. R. MOSES: *Identities* (1965)

DONALD PETERSEN: *The Spectral Boy* (1964)

MARGE PIERCY: *Breaking Camp* (1968)

HYAM PLUTZIK: *Apples from Shinar* (1959)

VERN RUTSALA: *The Window* (1964)

HARVEY SHAPIRO: *Battle Report* (1966)

JON SILKIN: *Poems New and Selected* (1966)

LOUIS SIMPSON: *At the End of the Open Road* (1963) [Pulitzer Prize in Poetry, 1964]; *A Dream of Governors* (1959)

JAMES WRIGHT: *The Branch Will Not Break* (1963); *Saint Judas* (1959); *Shall We Gather at the River* (1968)